Beginner Biography

Daniel Inouye

World War II Hero and Senator

by Jennifer Marino Walters
illustrated by Scott R. Brooks

Red Chair Press   Egremont, Massachusetts

Look! Books are produced and published by Red Chair Press:

Red Chair Press LLC   PO Box 333   South Egremont, MA 01258-0333

www.redchairpress.com

 FREE lesson guide at www.redchairpress.com/free-activities

Publisher's Cataloging-In-Publication Data

Names: Marino Walters, Jennifer, author. | Brooks, Scott R., illustrator.
Title: Daniel Inouye : World War II hero and senator / by Jennifer Marino Walters ; illustrated by Scott R. Brooks.

Description: Egremont, Massachusetts : Red Chair Press, [2020] | Series: Look! books. Beginner biography | Includes index, glossary, and resources for further reading. | Interest age level: 006-009. | Summary: "Daniel Inouye was born in Hawaii to parents who came from Japan. He had a happy life as a child until 1941 when the Japanese military bombed Pearl Harbor in his hometown. As war broke out, Daniel's life changed forever. He fought in the U.S. Army against the Japanese and then went on to serve Hawaii and his country in the U.S. Senate"--Provided by publisher.

Identifiers: ISBN 9781634407298 (library hardcover) | ISBN 9781634408967 (paperback) | ISBN 9781634408974 (ebook)

Subjects: LCSH: Inouye, Daniel K., 1924-2012--Juvenile literature. | Legislators--United States--Biography--Juvenile literature. | United States. Congress. Senate--Biography--Juvenile literature. | Japanese American soldiers--Hawaii--Biography--Juvenile literature. | World War, 1939-1945--Japanese Americans--Biography--Juvenile literature. | CYAC: Inouye, Daniel K., 1924-2012. | Legislators--United States--Biography. | United States. Congress. Senate--Biography. | Japanese American soldiers--Hawaii--Biography. | World War, 1939-1945--Japanese Americans--Biography.

Classification: LCC E840.8.I5 M37 2020 (print) | LCC E840.8.I5 (ebook) | DDC 328.73092 B--dc23

Library of Congress Control Number : 2019942456

Photo credits: p 4 and 22: The Daniel Inouye Institute

Printed in the United States of America

0420 1P CGF20

Table of Contents

Nisei

Daniel K. Inouye was born on September 7, 1924 in Honolulu, Hawaii. Daniel's parents had moved to the U.S. from Japan. That made Daniel a Nisei (nē-SAY)—a person born in the United States or Canada whose parents were Japanese **immigrants**.

Good to Know

Hawaii was a territory of the United States until 1959.

4

Honolulu is the state capital and on Oahu, one of six major islands of Hawaii.

Big Dreams

Daniel was the oldest of four children. His father worked two jobs to support the family. Daniel's parents taught him to always honor his country.

Young Daniel dreamed of being a doctor. He volunteered for the Red Cross in high school and planned to study medicine. But on December 7, 1941, everything changed.

A Surprise Attack

That morning, Japanese fighter planes attacked the U.S. naval base at Pearl Harbor, near Honolulu.

Japanese planes dropped bombs on American warships, sinking or damaging 19 of them. More than 2,000 U.S. service members and nearly 100 **civilians** died. Over 1,000 service members were wounded in the surprise attack.

Good to Know

The battleship USS *Arizona* remains **submerged** in shallow water off Pearl Harbor. Nearly two million people visit it each year.

9

World War II

The next day, the U.S. declared war on Japan and entered World War II. After Daniel graduated from high school, he tried to enlist in the U.S. military. But the U.S. government would not allow Nisei to fight for their country. Daniel enrolled in premedical studies at the University of Hawaii instead.

At the time, the U.S. government sent more than 100,000 Americans of Japanese **descent** to **internment camps** in the western U.S. In Hawaii, Japanese Americans had to follow **curfews.**

Joining the Military

In 1943, the U.S. ended its ban on Nisei serving in the military. Daniel left the University of Hawaii and joined the 442nd Regimental Combat Team. The unit was made up only of Japanese Americans. Many of them had been living in internment camps when they volunteered.

Good to Know

The 442nd Regimental Combat Team became the most highly decorated unit of its size in U.S. history. That means it received many awards and honors.

Bravery in Battle

Daniel spent four years with the 442nd. The team fought many tough battles in Italy and France. Daniel lost his right arm in one of the battles.

When Daniel left the Army in 1947, he received a Bronze Star and a Purple Heart. In 2000, he also received a Medal of Honor from President Bill Clinton for his bravery.

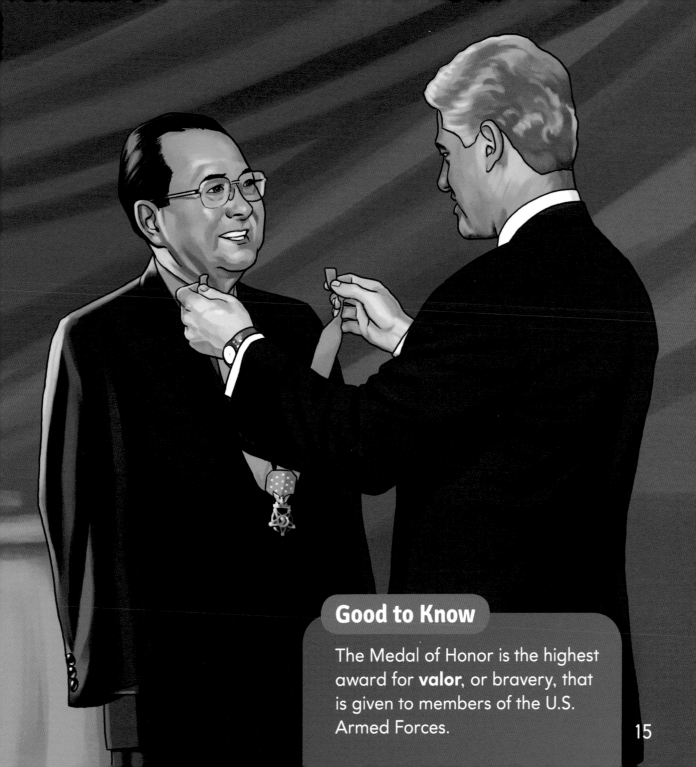

Good to Know

The Medal of Honor is the highest award for **valor**, or bravery, that is given to members of the U.S. Armed Forces.

Becoming a Politician

Daniel married Margaret Awamura in 1948. He graduated from the University of Hawaii in 1950, then went to law school. He became a lawyer in 1953.

In 1959, Hawaii became the 50th U.S. state. Daniel was chosen to be one of its first representatives in Congress. In 1962, he was elected to the U.S. Senate. That made him the first Japanese American ever to serve in the U.S. House of Representatives, and the first to serve in the U.S. Senate.

A Beloved Senator

As senator, Daniel helped to develop military sites in Hawaii. He also helped the state build modern transportation, schools, and communications systems. He fought for the rights of Hawaiians, Alaskans, and Native Americans.

Daniel's wife, Margaret, died in 2006. Then in 2008, he married Irene Hirano.

"Never underestimate the power of dreams."

Good to Know

Senator Inouye helped build a strong friendship between the U.S. and Japan.

Hawaii's Hero

Daniel was still a senator when he died on December 17, 2012 at age 88. That makes him the second longest serving member of the U.S. Senate. He is remembered for his heroism and hard work to improve the lives of Hawaiians and Japanese Americans.

Timeline: Big Dates in Daniel's Life

1924: Daniel is born in Honolulu, Hawaii.

1941: Japan attacks Pearl Harbor. The U.S. enters World War II.

1943: Daniel joins the 442nd Regimental Combat Team.

1947: Daniel leaves the Army. He receives a Bronze Star and a Purple Heart.

1948: He marries Margaret Awamura.

1959: Daniel becomes one of Hawaii's first representatives in Congress.

1962: He is elected to the U.S. Senate.

1964: Daniel's son, Kenny, is born.

2000: He is awarded the Medal of Honor by President Bill Clinton.

2006: Daniel's wife, Margaret, dies. He marries Irene Hirano two years later.

2012: Daniel dies at age 88.

Senator Inouye and his wife Irene

Words to Know

civilians: people who are not in the military

curfews: orders or laws requiring people to be at home by a certain time

descent: a person's line of ancestors

immigrants: people who come to a country to live there

internment camps: places where Japanese Americans were sent to live during World War II

submerged: covered with water

valor: bravery in the face of danger

Learn More at the Library

(Check out these books to read with others.)

Allen, Thomas. *Remember Pearl Harbor: American and Japanese Survivors Tell Their Stories.* National Geographic, 2015.

Mochizuki, Ken. *Baseball Saved Us.* Lee & Low, 1993.

Yamasaki, Katie. *Fish for Jimmy: Inspired by One Family's Experience in a Japanese American Internment Camp.* Holiday House, 2013.

Index

About the Author

Jennifer Marino Walters is married to a former service person who, like Senator Inouye, is of Japanese American descent. She and her husband live with their twin boys and daughter in the Washington D.C. area.